The Art of Defence in Bridge

Many players can bid a hand reasonably well, a good number can play the dummy for all it is worth, but very few excel in the art of defence. Good defence is not easy, for the defenders have to operate in the dark, without sight of each other's hands. Mistakes are bound to be numerous and costly unless the special techniques of defence have been studied.

In this book the authors cover all the main areas of defence in their usual lucid fashion, not only setting out the correct plays but explaining the reasoning behind each one. Having absorbed the lessons, the reader will find himself defeating more contracts than ever before.

The authors have won equal distinction as players and as writers on the game. For many years Roger Trézel was an automatic choice for the French International Team, as was Terence Reese for the British. Both were European and World Champions.

'. . . an excellent book in the Master Bridge Series. It is a well-written treatise covering the most difficult aspect of bridge. Well worth reading.'

– Derek Rimington, *Western Evening Herald*

D1584816

Terence Reese and Roger Trézel

The Art of Defence in Bridge

LONDON
VICTOR GOLLANCZ LTD
in association with Peter Crawley
1988

First published in 1979, reprinted 1984; reissued 1988
in association with Peter Crawley
by Victor Gollancz Ltd
14 Henrietta Street, London WC2E 8QJ

ISBN 0 575 02598 0

Printed in Great Britain by
St Edmundsbury Press Ltd, Bury St Edmunds, Suffolk

Introduction

by Terence Reese

The play of the cards at bridge is a big subject, capable of filling many large books. Some years ago Roger Trézel, the great French player and writer, had the idea of breaking up the game into several books of the present length, each dealing with one of the standard forms of technique. He judged, quite rightly as it turned out, that this scheme would appeal both to comparative beginners, who would be able to learn the game by stages, and to experienced players wishing to extend their knowledge of a particular branch of play.

We have now worked together on an English version, profiting from his experience.

The Art of Defence in Bridge

Defence is certainly the most difficult part of the game, because it calls for more imagination and experience than dummy play. It is seldom possible to form the sort of logical and comprehensive plan that is made by a declarer who can see twenty-six cards in combination. Nevertheless, defence has an extensive technique. We have aimed in this book to cover all the most important areas.

Contents

The Opening Lead

The first step in the defence, obviously, is the opening lead. Most players know the general principles involved and we do not propose to spend a lot of time on this subject—only to give some broad indications. In many cases the lead is a matter of guesswork: no one can say that one lead is better than another. Of course, certain holdings are more favourable than others. When you hold a strong sequence such as A K Q, K Q J, or Q J 10, or even a broken sequence such as A K J, K Q 10, or Q J 9, this suit is likely to be your choice because there is the double advantage that you are giving nothing away and may be establishing tricks for your own side. (The lead of the king from K Q 10, or the queen from Q J 9, is sometimes disastrous, of course, but one hopes to find partner with a supporting card.)

When no lead appears to stand out, we advise you to adopt a process of elimination. Say to yourself: 'I cannot lead this suit, for such and such a reason. Another suit is equally impossible, so the choice lies between the remaining two suits.' This negative approach may well bring you to the best answer.

Depending on whether the contract is no trumps or a suit, your objectives will be different. At no trumps it will usually be right to lead your longest suit, in the hope of establishing low cards. It is therefore quite normal to lead from suits headed by a combination such as A Q or K J. Against a suit contract you must have a good reason before you lead from this type of holding, because you risk giving a trick away for no good purpose. As a rule, safety is the paramount consideration. A trump lead, for example, will usually be safe, but it must be said that such a lead is apt to lose a tempo, to the extent that it permits the declarer to draw trumps and develop his own best side suit before you have attacked his weakness.

The lead of a singleton or doubleton will seldom give away a trick and may lead to a ruff. It is, however, most unwise to lead a singleton of declarer's side suit: you will too often kill a potential trick in your partner's hand.

The lead of your longest suit against a suit contract will generally be the best attack when you hold four trumps. (This applies when the declarer holds five trumps and his partner two or three; not so much when declarer holds four and the dummy four, because then declarer will play a crossruff game.) Your object is to force declarer to ruff so that eventually you will possess trump control.

It is normal to lead the higher card from a doubleton, the eight from 8 2. The lead from three cards, a combination such as 9 7 2, is a highly debatable problem. Some players lead the 9 ('top of nothing'), some the seven (the style known as MUD, signifying middle, up, down, as they intend to follow the seven with the nine), others the two, to make it clear that they hold three or more cards, not a doubleton. The top of nothing lead has gone out of fashion, because even after two rounds it may not be clear whether the leader has two cards or three. On the whole, we advise the low card, the two from 9 7 2, because at least this prevents partner from playing you for a doubleton. If you play with a regular partner, the lead from three cards is one of the first points to establish.

When you hold touching honours it is usual to lead the top card, the king from K Q 2, the queen from Q J 5, the jack from J 10 4. But when you hold three cards headed by a single honour or by honours not in sequence (for example, Q 10 x), lead the bottom card. The object is partly to distinguish the lead from a doubleton, still more to save a trick in many familiar situations, such as:

	8 4	
J 7 2		K 9 8 5 3
	A Q 10	

	9 5	
J 6 2		Q 8 7 4 3
	A K 10	

In each case the lead of the jack will present the declarer with three tricks. By leading the bottom card the defenders can hold declarer to two tricks, so long as the second lead is made by East.

These are similar examples:

	6 5	
Q 7 2		A 10 9 8 3
	K J 4	

	6 5	
Q 10 2		K 9 8 7 3
	A J 4	

A 6 2   J 10 9 8 4

K Q 3

Defending against no trumps, you must lead the bottom card in
each case, whether partner has bid the suit or not. Against a trump
contract it would not be wrong to lead the ace from A x x, but with
the other two holdings you should lead the two.

One of the problems in leading against a suit contract is that the
leader has to decide whether safety or aggression is the best policy.
This is a typical example:

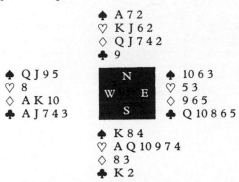

♠ A 7 2
♡ K J 6 2
◇ Q J 7 4 2
♣ 9

♠ Q J 9 5   ♠ 10 6 3
♡ 8   ♡ 5 3
◇ A K 10   ◇ 9 6 5
♣ A J 7 4 3   ♣ Q 10 8 6 5

♠ K 8 4
♡ A Q 10 9 7 4
◇ 8 3
♣ K 2

South plays in four hearts after West has doubled the opening bid
of one heart.

What should West lead? Most players would choose the king of
diamonds, because the lead is relatively safe, it contains attacking
possibilities, and it allows the leader to see the dummy and decide
what to play next. Yet on this occasion the king of diamonds gives
away the tempo: it allows declarer to establish diamonds before the
ace and king of spades have been forced out.

The winning lead is the queen of spades. Every player knows the sickening feeling of leading a queen and seeing K 10 x or A 10 x on the table, yet there is a sound reason for making this lead on the present occasion. West cannot hope for much in his partner's hand. East is more likely to hold the ten of spades than the queen of diamonds. And is there any *hurry* to lead a diamond? If declarer has three losers in the suit, how will he dispose of them when West controls both the spades and clubs? On the other hand, if the defence is to make a spade trick, he suit must be attacked at the first opportunity.

We do not say that the queen of spades will always turn out well. We say only that a good player would weigh all the chances and might settle on this card in preference to the more obvious king of diamonds.

To Cover or Not to Cover?

As a defender, when is it right to cover an honour card that has been led by the declarer? We all know the old saying, cover an honour with an honour, but that is far from being an answer to the problem.

In most situations it is correct to cover a *single* honour that has been led from your right. These are familiar examples:

Q 3 2

10 6 5   K 7 4

A J 9 8

When the queen is led from dummy, East must cover with the king to promote a trick for his partner's ten.

10 5 4

K 9 6   Q 3 2

A J 8 7

The ten is led from dummy and East must cover to ensure two tricks for his partner's K 9.

These are relatively simple plays, because the defender can see that dummy has only one honour. The best defence may not be so clear when the honour card is led from the closed hand.

A J 8 7

Q 3 2   6 5 4

K 10 9

When South leads the ten, should West cover? As the cards lie, to do so would save declarer a guess, but if partner held K 9 x it would be right to cover. Alas, there is no final answer to problems of this sort.

It is generally wrong to cover when there are two touching honours on your right:

Q J 9

10 6 4 2   K 8 5

A 7 3

When the queen is led from dummy, East must not cover on the first round, as this would expose his partner to a finesse and allow the declarer to make three tricks. Generally speaking, it is also wrong to cover when the queen is led from the closed hand in this type of situation:

A 7 3

K 8 5

queen led

Probably the declarer holds Q J and he may hold Q J 9. It is unlikely that the queen is unsupported, because then the normal play would be to lead towards it from the dummy.

Similarly, a defender must not cover when the jack is led from J 10 x:

J 10 2

K 8 7 3   Q 9 6

A 5 4

The jack is led from dummy and clearly it would cost a trick for East to cover. The same principle holds good when the lead is made from the closed hand:

A 8 7

Q 9 6

jack led

Here, West can hardly gain by covering the jack with the queen—or with the king if he holds K x x.

Some tricky problems may arise when a defender holds a doubleton honour. Consider East's position here, when the queen is led from dummy:

Q J 4 2

K 6

To cover with the king would be a mistake if South held A 9 8, correct if he held A x x x or A 9 x x. You cannot be right always, but in the long run the best policy is to cover with K 10 or K 9 but not with K x. The reason appears when the cards are like this:

Q J 4 2

10 8 5   K 6

A 9 7 3

The queen is led from dummy. Now, if you could see all the cards you would cover with the king. However, it would be wrong to cover if South held A 9 8, and the important point is that even if you do not cover on the present occasion it is by no means certain that you will lose your defensive trick. When the queen hods the first trick, declarer may well follow with the jack from dumlmy, aiming to pin a doubleton ten in the West hand. Against most opponents it would be good play for West to drop the eight on the first round, to create the impression that his holding was 10 8 alone.

Before leaving this subject, we must stress again that the object of covering an honour with an honour is to establish a lower card for yourself or your partner. If you keep that in mind you will avoid foolish plays in this type of position:

J 7 4 2

A   K 6 3

Q 10 9 8 5

South, who is marked with length in this suit, leads a tempting jack from the table. Great wailings when the king and ace fall together! Of course, it is idiotic for East to cover, as there is no possibility of promoting a low card.

A somewhat different example:

10 6 3

Q   J 9 8 5

A K 7 4 2

South, who has bid this suit, tries the deceptive lead of the ten from dummy. Heaven preserve us from partners who cover with the jack! When the queen falls on the same trick, South returns a low card to the six and eight, establishing a finesse position and so losing only one trick in the suit. To cover the ten with the jack in this situation is foolish because obviously South is not proposing to run the ten if his holding is A K Q x x.

Encouraging Signals

All bridge players who are beyond the novice stage are familiar with the standard ways of indicating strength: an unnecessarily high discard, usually the seven or above, or a high-low play, such as the five followed by the two. We propose to comment here on rather more advanced tactical situations. First, let us consider the right play with certain honour combinations.

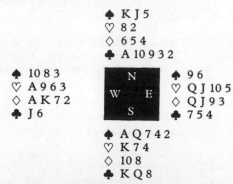

```
                    ♠ K J 5
                    ♡ 8 2
                    ◇ 6 5 4
                    ♣ A 10 9 3 2
    ♠ 10 8 3                        ♠ 9 6
    ♡ A 9 6 3          N            ♡ Q J 10 5
    ◇ A K 7 2       W     E         ◇ Q J 9 3
    ♣ J 6              S            ♣ 7 5 4
                    ♠ A Q 7 4 2
                    ♡ K 7 4
                    ◇ 10 8
                    ♣ K Q 8
```

South is in four spades and West leads the king of diamonds. From East's point of view, the club suit is ominous and he must realize that it may be essential for him to obtain the lead quickly and return the queen of hearts. The nine or jack of diamonds would be encouraging cards, it is true, but West might place East with a doubleton and so continue with the ace. The only correct card is the queen of diamonds. This conventionally denotes the Q J (or, of course, a singleton queen), so West will have no qualms about following with a low diamond to the jack. Then the queen of hearts will sink the declarer's ship.

Since the queen denotes the Q J, it follows that a defender must not play high-low from Q x. Nevertheless, it will often be clear to the opening leader that his partner holds a doubleton queen. For example:

```
                    J 8 5 3
    A K 10 6 2                      Q 4
                     9 7
```

Defending against a trump contract, West leads the king of the suit shown. When East plays the four and South the seven or nine, it is perfectly safe for West to follow with a low card. East must either hold Q x x or a singleton 4 or Q 4: he cannot hold 7 4 or 9 4, because with those cards he would have started a signal to show the doubleton.

Just as the queen is the right card from Q J, so the jack is played from J 10, denying the queen, while the ten denies the jack. These indications may be valuable at any time in the play.

7 5

A 9 8 4   J 10 6 2

K Q 3

Playing in a trump contract, declarer leads the five from dummy and it may well be correct for East to go in with the jack. When the king loses to the ace West knows that South holds the queen, since with Q J East, if playing an honour, would contribute the queen.

One of the most attractive manoeuvres open to the defenders is the false echo, designed to frighten the declarer into parting with a high trump which he cannot afford. Here is an example:

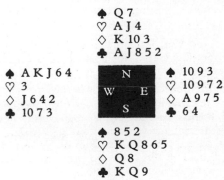

♠ Q 7
♡ A J 4
◇ K 10 3
♣ A J 8 5 2

♠ A K J 6 4   ♠ 10 9 3
♡ 3   ♡ 10 9 7 2
◇ J 6 4 2   ◇ A 9 7 5
♣ 10 7 3   ♣ 6 4

♠ 8 5 2
♡ K Q 8 6 5
◇ Q 8
♣ K Q 9

South plays in four hearts after West has overcalled in spades. West begins with the king and ace of spades, and East, realizing that the defence will probably need to make a trump trick in addition to two spades and a diamond, echoes with the ten and three of spades. When West follows with a third spade, South will probably be scared into ruffing with the jack of hearts. Having done so, he will not be able to avoid the loss of a trump to East's 10 9 x x.

Distributional Signals

There is an important difference between signals that show strength and signals that show distribution. For the most part, though there are exceptions both ways, a signal made when partner has led concerns strength, a signal on declarer's lead concerns distribution. A low card, when there is no reason to show strength, normally indicates an odd number of cards, a high card an even number.

These distributional signals are especially important when the declarer plays a suit in which dummy has length.

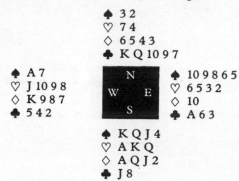

South is in 3NT and West leads the jack of hearts. It is not important here, but it is correct for East to prepare a small echo by dropping the three or five. He intends to follow with the two, and this will tell the opening leader that he holds four cards.

South wins with the king of hearts and leads the jack of clubs, on which West, holding an odd number, plays his lowest card, the two. South may attempt a small deception by overtaking with the queen, but East, having seen the two from his partner, will not be deceived. He will hold off this trick and will play the ace when declarer follows with the nine from dummy.

Sometimes a distributional signal will enable a defender to take his winner on the first round of a long suit. Suppose that a suit is divided as follows:

$$\begin{array}{ccc} & \text{K Q J 9 6 3} & \\ \text{8 7 4 2} & & \text{A 5} \\ & \text{10} & \end{array}$$

South leads the ten and plays the jack from dummy. On this trick West must drop the seven. Now, from East's angle, West may hold four cards, in which case it may be essential to take the ace at once, or West may hold a doubleton; if so, the suit cannot be shut out, so again East may as well play his ace on the first round.

In the trump suit itself a different convention applies. A player with J x or 10 x in the trump suit may not be able to spare the higher card on the first round, so convention requires him to play high-low with an odd number of cards, usually three, and to play his lowest card with an even number, two or four. The value of this signal is apparent on a deal of this kind:

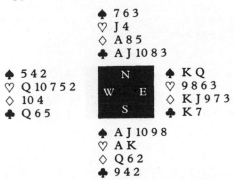

```
              ♠ 7 6 3
              ♡ J 4
              ◇ A 8 5
              ♣ A J 10 8 3
♠ 5 4 2                        ♠ K Q
♡ Q 10 7 5 2      N            ♡ 9 8 6 3
◇ 10 4        W       E        ◇ K J 9 7 3
♣ Q 6 5           S            ♣ K 7
              ♠ A J 10 9 8
              ♡ A K
              ◇ Q 6 2
              ♣ 9 4 2
```

South plays in four spades after opening one spade and rebidding the suit. West decides that the ten of diamonds is a more dynamic attack than a low heart. As the lead might be from K 10 9, and in any case to play the ace will not necessarily avert a ruff, South plays low from dummy. East wins and returns a diamond to dummy's ace. South now plays ace and another spade, and East is in.

East has to decide now whether to attempt to give partner a ruff in diamonds or to lead a heart, hoping to set up a trick in this suit before the clubs have been established. The key to the problem is West's play in the trump suit. West should play the five followed by the two, showing that he possesses a third trump. Then East will know what to do.

The trump echo—or, just as informative, the absence of a trump echo—will often help a defender to judge whether his side has trump control. In a contract of four hearts the trump suit is divided as follows:

$$\heartsuit\ 10\ 3$$

$$\heartsuit\ A\ 6 \qquad\qquad \heartsuit\ 9\ 7\ 5\ 4$$

$$\heartsuit\ K\ Q\ J\ 8\ 2$$

The declarer is forced to ruff at an early stage. He then plays a trump to the ten and a trump back, losing to the ace. Having seen his partner play the four and five of trumps, West can place him with an even number. If East began with four trumps, then by this time he will have as many trumps left as the declarer, and West will attempt to play a forcing game.

Suit-Preference Signals

One of the most valuable weapons in the defensive armoury is the suit-preference signal. When it is evident that the card played has no relation to a player's holding in the suit itself, then a high card suggests values in the higher-ranking of the suits other than trumps and the suit that has been led, a low card suggests values in the lower of the outstanding suits.

Perhaps the commonest use of the suit-preference signal occurs when a player is giving his partner a ruff and seeks at the same time to show where his re-entry lies.

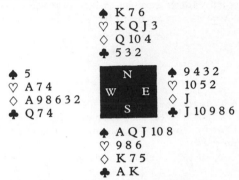

```
                    ♠ K 7 6
                    ♡ K Q J 3
                    ◇ Q 10 4
                    ♣ 5 3 2
    ♠ 5                                ♠ 9 4 3 2
    ♡ A 7 4          N                 ♡ 10 5 2
    ◇ A 9 8 6 3 2  W   E               ◇ J
    ♣ Q 7 4          S                 ♣ J 10 9 8 6
                    ♠ A Q J 10 8
                    ♡ 9 8 6
                    ◇ K 7 5
                    ♣ A K
```

South is in four spades and West leads the ace of diamonds. Seeing the fall of his partner's jack, he is hopeful of a singleton opposite and will naturally lead a second diamond. But how is he to tell his partner that he has a quick entry in hearts, not in clubs? He simply leads the nine of diamonds, an unnecessarily high card, at the second trick. This draws attention to the higher suit, hearts. Had his entry card been in clubs he would have led the two of diamonds.

Another opportunity for a signal of this kind occurs when the second card you play to a suit led by your partner can have no other significance.

```
                    ♡ 10 7 4
    ♡ A K J 8 2              ♡ 6 5 3
                    ♡ Q 9
```

Defending against a spade contract, West leads the king of hearts. East drops the three, which at this stage is a discouraging card, not a suit preference signal. West knows that it is safe to continue with the ace, and how East has an open choice between the five and the six, since he has already given the important message in this suit. If East wishes to suggest a switch to the lower suit, clubs, or has no particular preference, he will follow with the five, but if he would prefer a switch to diamonds he drops the six. Yes, an observant partner will notice the difference and may, indeed, complain bitterly if you fail to give the right signal.

Suit-preference signals are not so common at no trumps, but they may occur when following to partner's lead or when following to a suit being played by the declarer. For example, declarer plays off a suit of this type:

J 7 4 3

10 6 2   5

A K Q 9 8

When South leads the ace, West will follow naturally with the two. On the next two leads West may play the ten followed by the six, to convey to partner that he, West, can take care of the higher-ranking of the relevant suits. This may be very helpful to East, who has to make two discards before he has seen any discard by his partner.

It is true, of course, that there are technically three suits to consider apart from the one led, but in practice there is never the slightest difficulty in judging to which two suits the message relates. One suit will always be excluded by the bidding or previous play, or by the cards visible in dummy.

Ducking in Defence

Example 1

Another book in the present series deals entirely with ducking play by the declarer, and this form of play is almost equally valuable in defence. Of the examples that follow, the first is well known and relatively simple, except that on occasions a defender may have an awkward guess.

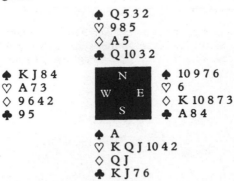

```
                    ♠ Q 5 3 2
                    ♡ 9 8 5
                    ◇ A 5
                    ♣ Q 10 3 2
    ♠ K J 8 4          N          ♠ 10 9 7 6
    ♡ A 7 3                       ♡ 6
    ◇ 9 6 4 2     W       E       ◇ K 10 8 7 3
    ♣ 9 5              S          ♣ A 8 4
                    ♠ A
                    ♡ K Q J 10 4 2
                    ◇ Q J
                    ♣ K J 7 6
```

The bidding goes:

SOUTH	WEST	NORTH	EAST
1 ♡	pass	1 ♠	pass
3 ♡	pass	4 ♡	pass
pass	pass		

West leads the nine of clubs. It would be good play for South to go up with the queen in dummy, tempting East to win. But East must recognize that his partner probably has a doubleton club and may well have an entry in the trump suit. To preserve communication, East must duck. Then West will have a second club to play when he wins with the ace of hearts.

The defence is easy on this deal because West is much more likely to hold a doubleton in clubs than a singleton. Sometimes it is impossible for a defender to know—particularly when there are four cards of the suit in dummy and the defender holds four himself. In these difficult situations it is wise to reflect that doubletons are more common than singletons.

Example 2

One of the commonest forms of ducking play occurs when the declarer is seeking to establish a long suit in dummy. It is often essential to hold up even when two controls are held.

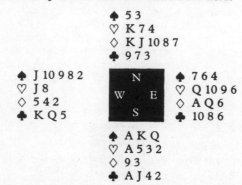

```
                    ♠ 5 3
                    ♡ K 7 4
                    ◇ K J 10 8 7
                    ♣ 9 7 3
    ♠ J 10 9 8 2        N        ♠ 7 6 4
    ♡ J 8                        ♡ Q 10 9 6
    ◇ 5 4 2       W       E      ◇ A Q 6
    ♣ K Q 5              S       ♣ 10 8 6
                    ♠ A K Q
                    ♡ A 5 3 2
                    ◇ 9 3
                    ♣ A J 4 2
```

South plays in 3NT and West leads the jack of spades. South wins and leads the nine of diamonds. East must not make the mistake of thinking that as he holds a second guard he can afford to win the first round. If East wins and returns a spade, South will have no difficulty in establishing the diamond suit. But if East holds off the first round of diamonds declarer will make just one trick in the suit instead of three.

The hold-up tends to be more difficult when the controlling cards are split between the two defenders. Suppose the diamond distribution here had been:

K J 10 8 7

A 5 2   Q 6 4

9 3

Again South runs the nine, and again East, to defeat the contract, must hold off. It is true that declarer might hold A 9 x, but with such a holding it is usual to play off the ace rather than finesse on the first round.

Moving into more expert territory, it may also be good play to hold up a jack in this type of situation. A suit is divided as follows:

K Q 10 8 7

6 5 2   A J 4

9 3

South leads the nine and takes the deep finesse. If dummy holds only one side entry, East should duck. South will repeat the finesse against the jack and now dummy's suit will be dead.

Plays of this type may also be correct when the defender sitting over the dummy holds Q x or J x. To duck now requires nerve, but the play will generally succeed.

Example 3

One of the most reliable principles in defensive play is this:
*Don't overruff an honour with an honour when there is a possibility
that refusing to overruff will bring in an extra trick in the trump suit.*

The principle is well known and most players would do the right
thing on this first example:

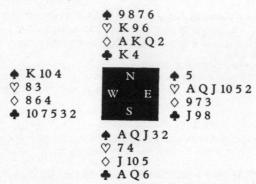

```
                    ♠ 9 8 7 6
                    ♡ K 9 6
                    ◇ A K Q 2
                    ♣ K 4
  ♠ K 10 4                          ♠ 5
  ♡ 8 3            N                ♡ A Q J 10 5 2
  ◇ 8 6 4      W       E            ◇ 9 7 3
  ♣ 10 7 5 3 2     S                ♣ J 9 8
                    ♠ A Q J 3 2
                    ♡ 7 4
                    ◇ J 10 5
                    ♣ A Q 6
```

South plays in four spades after East has overcalled in hearts.
West leads the eight of hearts and East wins with the ten. As there
is no prospect of a trick in the minor suits, East follows with ace
of hearts and another. Aware that an overruff is threatened, South
ruffs with the queen of spades.

It would be very amateurish now for West to overruff with the
king. All he need do is look the other way and discard a diamond.
Then his K 10 x, sitting over South's A J x x, will be worth two
tricks for sure.

On many occasions it will not be so clear, or so certain, that refusing to overruff will gain a trick. A defender has to take his partner's holding on trust.

6 3

J 7 4 2   K 8

A Q 10 9 5

At an early stage of the play South ruffs with the ten and West has a chance to overruff with the jack. He gains a trick by declining to do so.

This is another common position:

6 5 2

Q 8 4   K 9

A J 10 7 3

When South ruffs with the jack West may think it good business to overruff with the queen. But the play costs a trick!

It may also be wrong to overruff the hand that is short of trumps:

J

9 2   Q 8 6 4

A K 10 7 5 3

South ruffs a side suit with dummy's jack. If East overruffs, that will be his last trick in the trump suit. He must decline to overruff and then, thanks to partner's 9 x, his Q 8 x x is worth two tricks.

Example 4

We have been looking at examples where the refusal to overruff wins extra tricks by force of cards. Sometimes there is no extra trick to be won in the trump suit itself, but there is a strategical reason for rejecting the overruff.

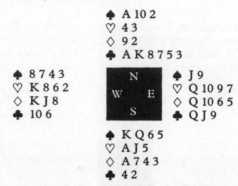

♠ A 10 2
♡ 4 3
◇ 9 2
♣ A K 8 7 5 3

♠ 8 7 4 3
♡ K 8 6 2
◇ K J 8
♣ 10 6

♠ J 9
♡ Q 10 9 7
◇ Q 10 6 5
♣ Q J 9

♠ K Q 6 5
♡ A J 5
◇ A 7 4 3
♣ 4 2

The best contract on the combined hands is 3NT, but South finishes in four spades. West leads the two of hearts, East plays the queen and South the ace. Declarer cannot hope to ruff his losers in the red suits and his likely plan is to establish the clubs. He plays ace, king and a low club, ruffing with the five of spades.

This is the critical moment of the deal. If West, happy to make a lowly trump, overruffs with the seven, he can do no further damage. Instead, he must discard from one of the red suits. Now declarer cannot draw trumps and run the clubs.

Having noted West's refusal to overruff, South may guess that the trumps are 4–2. Instead of attempting to draw trumps, he will probably exit with a diamond. Now the game for the defence is to lead trumps at each opportunity, because West has four trumps and South only three. South will be able to ruff a diamond with the ten of spades, but he will not be able to make a trick with the other low trump in his own hand. This way, he will end up with nine tricks, but no more.

Example 5

Imagine that the suit led against a no trump contract is divided in this way:

```
              Q 4
    10 9 3              A 8 7 6 2
              K J 5
```

When West leads the ten, East will of course duck, retaining his ace for eventual entry. Anyone who was not a complete beginner would make this play without hesitation. In many cases exactly the same principle applies, but the correct play is not so obvious.

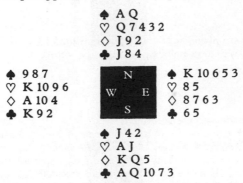

```
              ♠ A Q
              ♡ Q 7 4 3 2
              ◊ J 9 2
              ♣ J 8 4

♠ 9 8 7                      ♠ K 10 6 5 3
♡ K 10 9 6        N          ♡ 8 5
◊ A 10 4      W       E      ◊ 8 7 6 3
♣ K 9 2           S          ♣ 6 5

              ♠ J 4 2
              ♡ A J
              ◊ K Q 5
              ♣ A Q 10 7 3
```

Playing a strong no trump, South opens 1NT and the bidding continues:

SOUTH	WEST	NORTH	EAST
1NT	pass	2◊	pass
2♡	pass	3NT	pass
pass	pass		

Here North is using the system of transfer responses that is normal practice among tournament players. His bid of two diamonds signifies a heart suit, and when he goes to 3NT on the next round he tells his partner that he has a relatively balanced hand including five hearts.

West leads the nine of spades and the queen is played from dummy. If East pounces on this with the king, he destroys the defence. Lacking entries to his own hand, he must encourage with the six. West will come in at once with the king of clubs and lead a second spade to dummy's ace. Sooner or later the declarer must lose a trick in one of the red suits, and then the defence will be in a position to run three spade tricks.

If East were so misguided as to part with the king of spades at trick one, he might defend himself afterwards by saying: 'I would have looked foolish if I had held off and declarer had turned up with a doubleton J x.'

There are two answers to that. First, the contract would probably be defeated even if East presented the declarer with a second trick in spades. Second, the declarer was far more likely to hold J x x in spades rather than J x, since he had not only opened 1NT but had elected to play in no trumps even though his partner had shown a five-card suit of hearts.

Example 6

These hold-up plays in defence appear in many guises. If you had not met the situation before you might go wrong on the following deal:

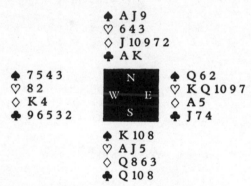

```
                    ♠ A J 9
                    ♡ 6 4 3
                    ♢ J 10 9 7 2
                    ♣ A K

        ♠ 7 5 4 3           N           ♠ Q 6 2
        ♡ 8 2                           ♡ K Q 10 9 7
        ♢ K 4           W       E       ♢ A 5
        ♣ 9 6 5 3 2         S           ♣ J 7 4

                    ♠ K 10 8
                    ♡ A J 5
                    ♢ Q 8 6 3
                    ♣ Q 10 8
```

The bidding goes:

SOUTH	WEST	NORTH	EAST
—	—	1◇	1♡
2NT	pass	3NT	pass
pass	pass		

West leads the eight of hearts, sitting East you play the queen and . . . But you are already lost! Declarer will duck this trick, win the next heart and play a diamond. West may go up with the king, but he has no heart to play.

The holding of K Q 10 9 7 requires the same treatment as A x x x x in the diagram at the beginning of Example 5. To leave his partner with a card to play when he gains the lead, East must put in the nine of hearts at trick one. South wins with the jack and plays on diamonds, but now West can go up with the king and lead a second heart, clearing the suit while his partner still has the ace of diamonds for entry.

There are many variations of this defensive play. Consider the following positions:

7 3

6 2   K Q J 8 4

A 10 9 5

South's bidding has suggested a double guard. When West leads the six it may be essential for East to play the eight, so that if West wins the first defensive trick he will have a second card to play.

K 8

6 3   A Q J 5 2

10 9 7 4

West leads the six and dummy plays the eight. It is tempting for East to play the jack, but if he has no outside entries it may be better to duck. Then if West can take a trick before South has made his contract, the defence will make four more tricks in the suit led.

Example 7

It is often necessary for the defenders to duck in the trump suit itself. An obvious example occurs when a trump is led by a defender and the suit is distributed in this fashion:

$$J\,9\,6\,2$$
$$8\,4 \qquad\qquad A\,10\,3$$
$$K\,Q\,7\,5$$

When a defender decides to lead a trump from a doubleton, it is usual to lead the lower card. (Occasionally the higher card will serve later for an overruff.) Here West leads the four of trumps and dummy plays low. Even if it is not clear from the bidding that declarer has only four trumps, East should duck. Then if West gains the first entry in a side suit he can lead a second trump and the defence can draw three rounds, which presumably is their tactical objective.

This is a typical hand where the defenders must contrive to get in three rounds of trumps before declarer can ruff in dummy:

♠ 9 8 4
♡ K 3
◊ K 7 4 3 2
♣ Q 5 4

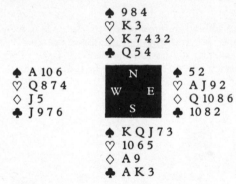

♠ A 10 6
♡ Q 8 7 4
◊ J 5
♣ J 9 7 6

♠ 5 2
♡ A J 9 2
◊ Q 10 8 6
♣ 10 8 2

♠ K Q J 7 3
♡ 10 6 5
◊ A 9
♣ A K 3

The bidding goes:

SOUTH	WEST	NORTH	EAST
1 ♠	pass	1NT	pass
2NT	pass	3 ♠	pass
4 ♠	pass	pass	pass

West leads the four of hearts, dummy plays low and East wins with the jack. East should judge that (a) his partner probably holds four hearts headed by the queen, (b) that the defence may need to take three tricks in hearts, and (c) that it is more important to attack trumps than clubs, because if declarer has a loser in clubs it won't run away.

East returns a trump, therefore, and South goes up with the king. West, appreciating the reason for his partner's trump return, must duck. South plays a second heart and now the defenders play two more rounds of spades. After this, the declarer will have no way to dispose of a third loser in hearts.

Clearly the defence would be lost if West played the ace on the first round of trumps and returned a trump. South would play another heart and would later ruff the third round.

Example 8

A defender who holds A x x x or K x x x in the trump suit should almost always hold up his control for one round, and very often for two rounds. Here West holds up the ace of trumps for two rounds so that he can exhaust dummy's trumps and force the declarer to ruff.

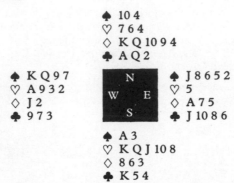

```
                    ♠ 10 4
                    ♡ 7 6 4
                    ◇ K Q 10 9 4
                    ♣ A Q 2
    ♠ K Q 9 7                      ♠ J 8 6 5 2
    ♡ A 9 3 2         N            ♡ 5
    ◇ J 2         W       E        ◇ A 7 5
    ♣ 9 7 3          S            ♣ J 10 8 6
                    ♠ A 3
                    ♡ K Q J 10 8
                    ◇ 8 6 3
                    ♣ K 5 4
```

South is in four hearts and West leads the king of spades. As a switch to diamonds would threaten a ruff, South wins the first trick and plays on trumps, intending to force out the ace. West must decline to win both the first and second round of trumps, because if he does so there will still be a trump in dummy to take care of spade leads.

When South is allowed to hold the first two tricks in hearts he is in a quandary. If he plays a third trump the defence will win and continue spades. South will then run out of steam, for if he ruffs the third spade and draws the outstanding trump he will have no hearts left when the defenders come in with the ace of diamonds. Alternatively, South may broach diamonds when he finds the trumps 4—1, but this allows the defence to score a diamond ruff.

Oddly enough, it is easier for East to make a critical error than West. Noting West's two of hearts on the first round, he must place his partner with four hearts (with three West would have begun an echo) and keep enough spades to embarrass the declarer at a later stage. In fact, East's first two discards must be precisely a spade and a club. He must not let go a diamond, because then declarer can play on diamonds without incurring a ruff.

You see why it is fatal for East to let go two spades? South can force out the ace of hearts, ruff the third round of spades, draw the last trump, and lead a diamond. When East comes in with the ace of diamonds he will have no spade to play.

Example 9

A defender who holds A x x x of the trump suit should always have
in mind the possibility of weakening the declarer's trump holding.
To achieve this, it may be necessary to present the declarer with a
ruff-and-discard. The defence on the following deal is quite simple:

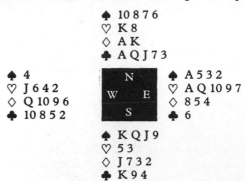

```
                    ♠ 10 8 7 6
                    ♡ K 8
                    ◇ A K
                    ♣ A Q J 7 3
   ♠ 4                 N          ♠ A 5 3 2
   ♡ J 6 4 2      W        E      ♡ A Q 10 9 7
   ◇ Q 10 9 6                     ◇ 8 5 4
   ♣ 10 8 5 2         S           ♣ 6
                    ♠ K Q J 9
                    ♡ 5 3
                    ◇ J 7 3 2
                    ♣ K 9 4
```

The bidding goes:

SOUTH	WEST	NORTH	EAST
—	—	1♣	1♡
1♠	pass	3♠	pass
4♠	pass	pass	pass

West leads the two of hearts and East makes the first two tricks
with the queen and ace. Now it should be apparent to East (a)
that if South has only four spades his trump position if open to
attack, and (b) that a ruff-and-discard will not help the declarer,
as he cannot have any losers in the minor suits. East, therefore,
launches an attack on declarer's trump holding by playing a heart
at trick three.

Suppose that South takes the force in dummy and plays on trumps.
East holds off for two rounds, leaving the cards as follows:

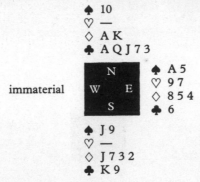

```
                    ♠ 10
                    ♡ —
                    ◇ A K
                    ♣ A Q J 7 3

                    N            ♠ A 5
    immaterial    W   E          ♡ 9 7
                    S            ◇ 8 5 4
                                 ♣ 6
                    ♠ J 9
                    ♡ —
                    ◇ J 7 3 2
                    ♣ K 9
```

South is now in a hopeless position. If he plays on clubs he allows
East to make his small trump, and if he continues spades he will
go two down, as East in due course will make ace of spades, a low
spade and his fifth heart.

Example 10

We return now to problems of communication that arise in no trump contracts. The deal below occurred in a team-of-four match. At one table North was the declarer in 3NT, at the other table South. This should have made no difference, but it did.

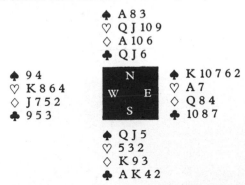

♠ A 8 3
♡ Q J 10 9
◇ A 10 6
♣ Q J 6

♠ 9 4
♡ K 8 6 4
◇ J 7 5 2
♣ 9 5 3

♠ K 10 7 6 2
♡ A 7
◇ Q 8 4
♣ 10 8 7

♠ Q J 5
♡ 5 3 2
◇ K 9 3
♣ A K 4 2

At the first table South opened one club and North responded 3NT, which was passed out. The play followed a normal course. East led the six of spades and dummy's jack held the trick. A low heart was led from the table and West made the excellent play of going up with the king to protect his partner's entry. A second spade from the West side now spelt doom for the declarer, the defence making three spades and two hearts.

At the other table North scientifically responded one heart to the opening one club, so South became the declarer after this auction:

SOUTH	WEST	NORTH	EAST
1♣	pass	1♡	1♠
pass	pass	2♠	pass
2NT	pass	3NT	pass
pass	pass		

West led the nine of spades, East won with the king and returned a spade. Now the defenders could not achieve the same sequence as at the first table, because even if West had won the first round of hearts he would not have been able to lead a spade. South made ten tricks without difficulty.

You see what went wrong? East must duck the first round of spades. As North is now the exposed hand it is quite easy for West to go up with the king of hearts on the first round of this suit and lead his second spade, defeating the contract in the same way as before.

Example 11

It is often possible, in defence, to persuade the declarer to part with a high card which he would do better to hold up. The commonest occasion for this tactical play by the defence occurs on this type of hand:

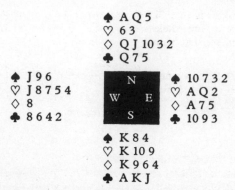

```
              ♠ A Q 5
              ♡ 6 3
              ◇ Q J 10 3 2
              ♣ Q 7 5
♠ J 9 6                        ♠ 10 7 3 2
♡ J 8 7 5 4      N             ♡ A Q 2
◇ 8           W     E          ◇ A 7 5
♣ 8 6 4 2         S            ♣ 10 9 3
              ♠ K 8 4
              ♡ K 10 9
              ◇ K 9 6 4
              ♣ A K J
```

South is in 3NT and West leads the five of hearts. It is easy to see what will happen if East wins with the ace and follows with the queen: South will hold up until the third round and West's long hearts will wither on the vine.

The correct play on the first trick is the queen of hearts. It is now almost impossible for South to duck. He would look especially foolish if West held four hearts headed by the ace, for then the defence would take four hearts and a diamond, defeating a lay-down contract.

This type of play is simple with A Q x, because the declarer in a no trump contract will surely not hold a singleton king. The situation is more delicate when East can see the following cards:

6 3

5 led   A J 2

Here it is dangerous in a way to play the jack, because declarer may hold only Q x x. Nevertheless, the jack tends to be the better play when East can see that his partner can hold very little, and certainly no side entry.

When dummy holds a singleton, the finesse against partner is still more likely to be the correct play.

7

A 9 6 5 3   K J 4

Q 10 8 2

Suppose here that the critical side entry lies with West. If East plays the king on the first round and returns the jack, South will cover with the queen and it will be impossible now for the defence to establish four tricks. (West may duck, but East has no quick entry.) If East plays the jack on the first lead, the declarer is lost whether he ducks or wins with the queen, because the defenders will have better communication.

Example 12

How would you fancy the declarer's chances in 3NT on this next hand?

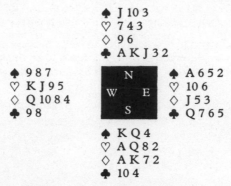

```
                    ♠ J 10 3
                    ♡ 7 4 3
                    ◇ 9 6
                    ♣ A K J 3 2
    ♠ 9 8 7              N              ♠ A 6 5 2
    ♡ K J 9 5                           ♡ 10 6
    ◇ Q 10 8 4       W       E          ◇ J 5 3
    ♣ 9 8                S              ♣ Q 7 6 5
                    ♠ K Q 4
                    ♡ A Q 8 2
                    ◇ A K 7 2
                    ♣ 10 4
```

As South was playing a weak no trump when not vulnerable, he opened one heart and the bidding proceeded:

SOUTH	WEST	NORTH	EAST
1 ♡	pass	2 ♣	pass
3NT	pass	pass	pass

West led the four of diamonds. On the surface, South has two spade tricks, four in clubs, two in diamonds and one in hearts. But there were entry problems, and these were cleverly exploited by the defenders.

South captured the jack of diamonds with his king and ran the ten of clubs. East calmly played low. Suspicious of the club situation, South did not repeat the finesse but led the king of spades. Again, East refused to win. South continued with the queen of spades, and, for the third time, East held off. Now there was no play for the contract.

You may think that East could have achieved the same result by winning the queen of spades and playing a third round, to kill dummy's entry. This gives declarer a chance, if he reads the position correctly. He cashes ace and king of clubs, forcing West to discard a heart. He follows with the ace and another diamond, and after cashing his diamond winners West is forced to lead a heart into the declarer's A Q. This way, South makes two tricks in spades, two in hearts, two in diamonds and three in clubs.

East ducked three times in the play of this hand, each time for a different reason. The duck on the first round of clubs prevented South from running four club tricks. The duck of the king of spades prevented South from entering dummy later with the jack of spades, and the duck on the second round of spades was necessary to maintain a link between the defending hands and so prevent West from being end-played.

Example 13

One of the commonest errors in defence is to win with a high card when it would be more economical to retain the control. A very simple example occurs when declarer, holding K x x opposite Q x x, leads low to the queen. Obviously, the play of the ace by the second player would present declarer with a second trick. Few players would make this mistake, but a large number would make the wrong play on the following deal and would argue afterwards that their play was correct.

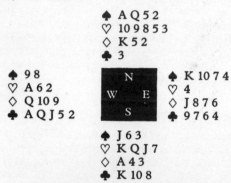

```
              ♠ A Q 5 2
              ♡ 10 9 8 5 3
              ◇ K 5 2
              ♣ 3
♠ 9 8                      N              ♠ K 10 7 4
♡ A 6 2                                   ♡ 4
◇ Q 10 9             W         E          ◇ J 8 7 6
♣ A Q J 5 2                S              ♣ 9 7 6 4
              ♠ J 6 3
              ♡ K Q J 7
              ◇ A 4 3
              ♣ K 10 8
```

South opens one heart, West overcalls with two clubs, and North bids four hearts. Vulnerable against not, East decides against a sacrifice, so four hearts becomes the final contract.

West leads the nine of spades. Declarer plays low from dummy, East wins with the king and . . .

Too late! By abandoning his double stop in spades, East has allowed South to make three tricks in the suit. One of his diamonds will go away on the fourth spade and he will lose just one spade, one heart and one club.

If there is any criticism of his play East will argue:
(1) That the lead might have been a singleton. This is possible, but less likely than a doubleton for a number of reasons. Also, if East wins with the king and returns a spade for his partner to ruff, West will be ruffing a loser and there may be no gain for the defence.
(2) That the lead might be from 9 8 x, declarer holding J x alone. But then again it is doubtful whether to win with the king will achieve anything. Dummy's A Q of spades will take care of losing diamonds, and four tricks will be hard to find.

It is often good play to hold up an honour card even when it seems that the winner may be lost for ever. Suppose that either at no trumps or in a suit contract the distribution of the suit led is as follows:

A Q 7 5

10 9 8 4 3   K 6

J 2

When West leads the ten and dummy plays low, East should normally play the six. If he parts with the king he sets up three certain winners for the declarer. If he plays low the odds are that declarer, seeking to establish three winners, will finesse again. Of course, this type of hold-up can go wrong, but a defender should at least be prepared to make it without any revealing hesitation.

Example 14

One of the surest marks of a weak player is that he will always
come to the aid of the declarer when it is necessary to guess a
K J situation. Everyone is familiar with this type of position:

K J 7 5

A 9 6 4   Q 10 3

8 2

South leads low and West, fearing that South may hold a singleton
and may be intending to go up with the king, will rush in with the
ace. Now it must be admitted that sometimes the declarer will hold
a singleton and it may be fatal to lose the trick. Nobody can guess
right every time, but in general it is better to steel yourself to play
low. After all, the declarer may finesse the jack if he thinks that
West holds the queen and East the ace. It will depend on whether
he needs to set up a discard, and these positions are not too
difficult to read.

Players who habitually play their aces in front of dummy's K J
solve the declarer's problem when they hold only the queen.
South can say to himself: 'If West had held the ace he would have
played it, so I will finesse against the queen.'

A defender has a more difficult problem when he can see the
singleton in dummy. The suit may be divided in this fashion:

6

Q 9 4 3   A 8 7 5 2

K J 10

East must be prepared for the lead of the singleton which he can
see on the table. Whether it is right to go up with the ace or to
play low will depend on whether dummy has a loser that can
profitably be discarded on the king of the suit that has been led.

To reinforce the lesson, here is a deal where the defender knows that dummy has a singleton and that declarer has K Q, and it is still best play to duck:

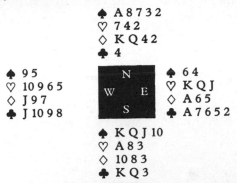

♠ A 8 7 3 2
♥ 7 4 2
♦ K Q 4 2
♣ 4

♠ 9 5
♥ 10 9 6 5
♦ J 9 7
♣ J 10 9 8

♠ 6 4
♥ K Q J
♦ A 6 5
♣ A 7 6 5 2

♠ K Q J 10
♥ A 8 3
♦ 10 8 3
♣ K Q 3

South is in four spades and West leads the jack of clubs. It is clear from a sight of all the cards, and should be clear to East at trick one, that to part with the ace of clubs will make the play simple. South will later discard two hearts on the K Q of clubs and will lose just two diamonds and one club.

So East must play low on the opening lead. South wins with the king, and if a good player he will continue as follows: club ruff, spade to king, club ruff, spade to queen, ace and another heart. East makes two heart tricks and must then exit with a low diamond. This way, the defenders still make two tricks in diamonds, defeating the contract.

Example 15

It is sometimes necessary not merely to refuse to win a trick, but at the same time to dispose of a card that might win a trick later.

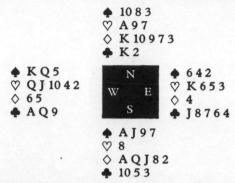

```
              ♠ 10 8 3
              ♡ A 9 7
              ◇ K 10 9 7 3
              ♣ K 2
♠ K Q 5                      ♠ 6 4 2
♡ Q J 10 4 2      N          ♡ K 6 5 3
◇ 6 5        W       E       ◇ 4
♣ A Q 9          S           ♣ J 8 7 6 4
              ♠ A J 9 7
              ♡ 8
              ◇ A Q J 8 2
              ♣ 10 5 3
```

South played in five diamonds and West led the queen of hearts to dummy's ace. South ruffed a heart, drew one round of trumps, and led a low club. Not seeing that it could make any difference, West went up with the ace of clubs and led a trump. South won in dummy, cashed the king of clubs, ruffed a heart and ruffed the third club. Then he played the 10 of spades from dummy. West won with the queen and was unable to exit without giving South an extra trick. It was a simple elimination ending.

Let's go back to the point at which the low club was led:

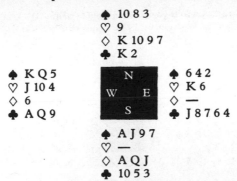

```
                    ♠ 10 8 3
                    ♡ 9
                    ◇ K 10 9 7
                    ♣ K 2
    ♠ K Q 5          N          ♠ 6 4 2
    ♡ J 10 4                    ♡ K 6
    ◇ 6          W       E      ◇ —
    ♣ A Q 9                     ♣ J 8 7 6 4
                    S
                    ♠ A J 9 7
                    ♡ —
                    ◇ A Q J
                    ♣ 10 5 3
```

West fares no better if he plays a low club instead of the ace: declarer can achieve the same end-play. West must play the *queen* of clubs. Then East can win the second round of the suit and lead a spade. West wins with the queen and exits with the ace of clubs. South ruffs in dummy and has no alternative but to try a second finesse in spades.

Example 16

One of the most subtle ways of refusing to win a trick is by underruffing in the trump suit. The play was not too difficult on this deal:

```
                    ♠ A Q 10
                    ♡ 6 4 2
                    ◇ 9 7 5
                    ♣ A J 4 2
   ♠ 8 6 4 3           N           ♠ 9 7 5
   ♡ K 10 8 5                       ♡ —
   ◇ 3 2          W         E       ◇ A Q J 10 8
   ♣ Q 10 5           S           ♣ K 9 8 6 3
                    ♠ K J 2
                    ♡ A Q J 9 7 3
                    ◇ K 6 4
                    ♣ 7
```

East opened one diamond, South overcalled with two hearts, and North raised to four hearts. East, who was vulnerable, decided not to venture five clubs and West refrained from doubling, so four hearts became the final contract.

West led the three of diamonds and East, not liking the spade situation, decided that the best chance would be to find his partner with a singleton diamond. He went up with the ace and returned a diamond. South won, entered dummy with a spade, and led a low heart from the table. When East showed out, South played the ace.

50

Faced with the possible loss of two trumps and two diamonds, South tried to make additional tricks by ruffing clubs. He played a club to the ace, ruffed a club, entered dummy with a spade and ruffed another club. After a third round of spades the position was:

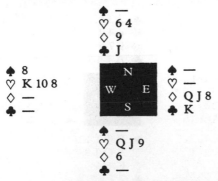

```
              ♠ —
              ♡ 6 4
              ◇ 9
              ♣ J
   ♠ 8                    ♠ —
   ♡ K 10 8     N         ♡ —
   ◇ —       W   E        ◇ Q J 8
   ♣ —          S         ♣ K
              ♠ —
              ♡ Q J 9
              ◇ 6
              ♣ —
```

On the next club East played the king and South ruffed with the queen of hearts. If West takes this trick with the king, obviously South will make two more tricks with the J 9. Equally, if West discards a spade the defence will be lost, for West will be obliged to ruff a diamond on the next trick. Instead, West must underruff with the eight of hearts. East wins the next trick, and West is left with the K 10 of hearts over South's J 9.

Example 17

There is one quite different situation where to underruff is the only play. If you achieve at the table the coup described below, you will not have lived in vain.

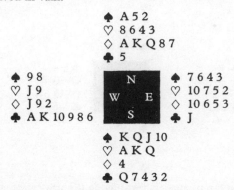

```
              ♠ A 5 2
              ♡ 8 6 4 3
              ◇ A K Q 8 7
              ♣ 5
  ♠ 9 8                        ♠ 7 6 4 3
  ♡ J 9          N             ♡ 10 7 5 2
  ◇ J 9 2     W     E          ◇ 10 6 5 3
  ♣ A K 10 9 8 6    S          ♣ J
              ♠ K Q J 10
              ♡ A K Q
              ◇ 4
              ♣ Q 7 4 3 2
```

The contract of six spades by South is not easy to reach. With North the dealer, this is a possible route:

SOUTH	NORTH
—	1 ◇
2 ♣	2 ◇
2 ♠	3 ♡
3NT	4 ♠
6 ♠	pass

West leads the king of clubs and, seeing his partner's jack, follows with a low club. Taking no chances, South ruffs with the ace of spades.

Though East may not realize it, this is the critical point of the deal. Obviously he must not let go a diamond, it may not occur to him to 'discard' a trump, so he will probably let go a heart. This proves a fatal discard, for South makes the slam easily by way of four spade tricks, a ruff with the ace of spades, three diamonds and four hearts.

'That was funny. I was squeezed at trick two', says East.

Precisely—but he could have averted the evil day for ever by underruffing. Declarer is left with menace cards against East in hearts and diamonds, but he can do nothing with them. This is the end position:

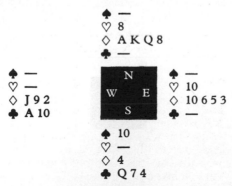

South leads the ten of spades, but East is not embarrassed, since dummy has to make the first discard.

It is a well known principle of squeeze play that nothing can be achieved when both menaces (in this case the fourth heart and the fourth diamond) are 'under' the player who controls them. For this reason, it does not require superhuman skill for East to avert the possible squeeze by underruffing on the second trick. And if East fails to do this, and gets the blame, he can always point out that a diamond from West at trick two would be a simple and effective defence.

Example 18

You will defeat many contracts, in quite an unexpected way, if you follow this principle of defence:

Be very reluctant to part with controlling cards in declarer's long side suit.

Sometimes this form of play will cause the declarer to follow a completely wrong line. Suppose that a side suit is divided as follows:

```
                    6 3
    K 8 7 4                    J 2
                  A Q 10 9 5
```

Declarer finesses the queen. If West wins, the rest of the play may be simple. Suppose, instead, that West ducks. South will cash the ace and follow with the ten. Expecting the king to fall from East, he will ruff low in dummy. East will overruff, the suit is still not established, and the contract may be in ruins.

On the following hand South is not deceived, but the defenders can beat the contract by a series of clever moves.

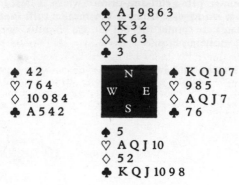

```
                    ♠ A J 9 8 6 3
                    ♡ K 3 2
                    ◇ K 6 3
                    ♣ 3
    ♠ 4 2                              ♠ K Q 10 7
    ♡ 7 6 4            N               ♡ 9 8 5
    ◇ 10 9 8 4      W     E            ◇ A Q J 7
    ♣ A 5 4 2          S               ♣ 7 6
                    ♠ 5
                    ♡ A Q J 10
                    ◇ 5 2
                    ♣ K Q J 10 9 8
```

South is in four hearts and the defenders start with three rounds of diamonds, forcing South to ruff. South leads the king of clubs and West, knowing that declarer has length in clubs, declines to part with the ace. South follows with the queen of clubs and West ducks again. On the jack of clubs West plays low, dummy discards, and East ruffs. The position is now:

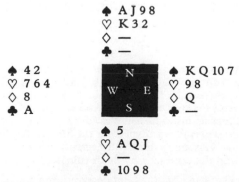

```
              ♠ A J 9 8
              ♡ K 3 2
              ◇ —
              ♣ —
 ♠ 4 2                        ♠ K Q 10 7
 ♡ 7 6 4        N            ♡ 9 8
 ◇ 8        W       E        ◇ Q
 ♣ A            S            ♣ —
              ♠ 5
              ♡ A Q J
              ◇ —
              ♣ 10 9 8
```

East completes the defence by leading a diamond at this point, presenting South with a ruff-and-discard which is fatal to him because he has inadequate trumps. Whether he ruffs in dummy or in his own hand, he cannot ruff out the ace of clubs, draw trumps and cash the winning clubs.*

* There is a very similar hand in my book, *The Expert Game,* but I could see no reason not to repeat the example here. The play is certainly more advanced than the majority in the present book, but the basic principle—hang on to your controls in the long side suit—is easy to understand.—T.R.

Blocking and Unblocking Plays in Defence

Blocking and unblocking plays are as common in defence as in attack, but they tend to be of a different nature because of the different angle from which the dummy is viewed. The first example below is more associated with the play of the defenders than of the declarer.

Example 1

The defenders at no trumps will often establish a suit in the first two or three leads, but the player with the long suit may still require an entry to run off his winners. When the entry lies in the declarer's own long suit, an imaginative unblock may be necessary.

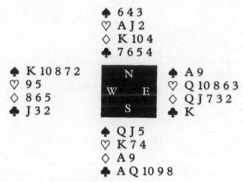

```
                    ♠ 6 4 3
                    ♡ A J 2
                    ◇ K 10 4
                    ♣ 7 6 5 4
  ♠ K 10 8 7 2        N         ♠ A 9
  ♡ 9 5                         ♡ Q 10 8 6 3
  ◇ 8 6 5       W        E      ◇ Q J 7 3 2
  ♣ J 3 2            S          ♣ K
                    ♠ Q J 5
                    ♡ K 7 4
                    ◇ A 9
                    ♣ A Q 10 9 8
```

South opens 1NT, North raises to 2NT, and South goes to 3NT on the strength of his five-card suit.

West leads the seven of spades, East wins with the ace and returns the nine. As it is apparent that East cannot have a third spade, West wins with the king and clears the suit by leading the two. He chooses the two to direct his partner's attention to his only possible re-entry card, which is in the lowest suit, clubs.

Even without this indication, East should recognize that the lone king of clubs has no value in itself and may, indeed, prove an obstruction. He should seize the opportunity to dispose of this card on the third round of spades. Then South cannot establish his clubs without letting West into the lead, and the defence will make four tricks in spades and one in clubs.

You may think that West's jack of clubs would in any event be an entry, since the declarer, knowing West to be the danger hand, might begin by playing off the ace of clubs. But that would not in fact be good play. After winning the third spade South should enter dummy with a diamond or a heart and lead a club from the table. If East plays low, South intends to play the ace (a safety play lest West hold the singleton king), but when the king appears from East, South allows it to win.

Note that the same type of unblock would be necessary if East held a singleton queen. In some cases it may even be advisable to jettison a singleton ace, to ensure entry for a partner who may hold J x x or Q x.

Example 2

When an ace or king is led, a defender must always be alert to the possibility of dropping a lower honour. This is sometimes a good deceptive play, as when a suit is divided in this fashion:

Q 10 7 4 2

K 6   J 9 3

A 8 5

Proposing to establish this suit in a no trump contract, South leads the ace. West can see that prospects for his side are poor, and to mislead the declarer he drops the king from K x. If South has not met this type of play before he may assume that East holds J 9 x x and may seek to develop his tricks elsewhere.

Generally speaking, if you know that an honour card is going to fall on the next round, achieving no good purpose, it is good tactics to play it a round earlier than is necessary. Take this simple position:

A 5 4

10 6 2   Q 8 7

K J 9 3

It is clear that South has four tricks for the asking, but the defenders can spin a deceptive web. When the three is led from hand, West drops the six. South plays the ace from dummy and returns the four. On this trick East plays the queen, South the king, and West the two. The combined effect of the queen from East on the second round, and the echo by West, suggesting four cards, may well persuade the declarer that the suit is not breaking. The play is much the same when West holds Q x x in front of dummy's K J x x.

On this next deal West's unblocking play ensures an entry for his partner, and there is nothing the declarer can do about it:

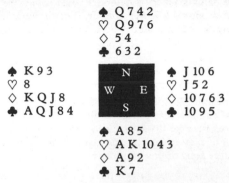

```
                  ♠ Q 7 4 2
                  ♡ Q 9 7 6
                  ◇ 5 4
                  ♣ 6 3 2

    ♠ K 9 3          N          ♠ J 10 6
    ♡ 8         W         E     ♡ J 5 2
    ◇ K Q J 8                   ◇ 10 7 6 3
    ♣ A Q J 8 4       S         ♣ 10 9 5

                  ♠ A 8 5
                  ♡ A K 10 4 3
                  ◇ A 9 2
                  ♣ K 7
```

South opens one heart, West doubles, and North raises defensively to two hearts. Although this is a weak bid after the take-out double, South has enough to bid four hearts.

West leads the king of diamonds and South plays correctly by ducking. (Otherwise, East's ten of diamonds would become a possible entry card.) West continues with a second high diamond, and after drawing trumps South leads the ace of spades. At this point West must not fail to drop the king. Then South cannot establish dummy's long spade without letting East into the lead to play a club.

Note that South would fare no better by leading a low spade on the first round. Dummy's queen wins and on the next round West can drop the king under the ace.

Declarer's best line, actually, is to lead a low spade while dummy still has a trump entry. Suppose that West held K 10 x of spades and East J 9 x. Then West would need to insert the ten on the first round, and this is quite a difficult play. If West, holding K 10 x, plays low, the queen wins and a low spade is returned. East may go in with the jack, but then South will play the ace and West will still have to win the third round.

Example 3

Blocking plays in defence generally take the form of 'second hand high'. The object may be to prevent an entry-finesse. This is a common situation:

A J 6 3

K 8 7 5   10 9 2

Q 4

Needing entries to dummy, perhaps for a finesse in the trump suit, declarer leads the four, intending to finesse the jack. West can frustrate him by playing the king on the first round.

Sometimes a big card by the second player will interrupt the declarer's communications:

A K 10 9 3 2

J 5   Q 7 4

8 6

Suppose that the declarer in a no trump contract wants to establish this suit but cannot afford to let West obtain the lead. Lacking a side entry to the dummy, he leads low, intending to duck the trick to East. The play of the jack by West spoils this plan. South does not want to let West win the trick, and if he plays high from dummy his communications will be ruined. The same play is sometimes indicated when a defender holds K x in front of dummy's A Q 10 x x x.

The play of the club suit on the following deal has interesting variations:

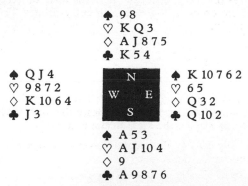

```
                    ♠ 9 8
                    ♡ K Q 3
                    ◇ A J 8 7 5
                    ♣ K 5 4
♠ Q J 4                              ♠ K 10 7 6 2
♡ 9 8 7 2              N              ♡ 6 5
◇ K 10 6 4         W     E            ◇ Q 3 2
♣ J 3                 S              ♣ Q 10 2
                    ♠ A 5 3
                    ♡ A J 10 4
                    ◇ 9
                    ♣ A 9 8 7 6
```

South is in 3NT, and as hearts have been bid West leads the queen of spades. Declarer holds up until the third round, and from the play of the cards he judges that East is the danger hand with the long spades.

Hoping to establish the clubs without letting East into the lead, South may cross to dummy in hearts and lead a low club from the table. Now East must be sufficiently alert to play the ten, to prevent declarer from ducking the trick to West.

The defence is more difficult if South plays the king of clubs on the first round and follows with a low club from dummy. Now East must play the 'crocodile coup', opening his jaws and playing the queen of clubs, to swallow his partner's jack. East, of course, does not know that his partner holds the jack, but he must assume that if South holds A J he will finesse, so the play of the queen will not cost.

Trump Promotion and the Uppercut

On numerous occasions the defenders are able to promote trump tricks which would be beyond their reach if the declarer were able to draw a round or two of trumps early on. One of the best known weapons is the 'uppercut'.

Example 1

To earn its name, the uppercut consists of the ruff of a winning card with a trump that forces the declarer to expend a valuable card when he overruffs.

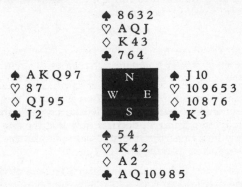

```
              ♠ 8 6 3 2
              ♡ A Q J
              ◇ K 4 3
              ♣ 7 6 4
♠ A K Q 9 7      N        ♠ J 10
♡ 8 7                     ♡ 10 9 6 5 3
◇ Q J 9 5      W   E      ◇ 10 8 7 6
♣ J 2            S        ♣ K 3
              ♠ 5 4
              ♡ K 4 2
              ◇ A 2
              ♣ A Q 10 9 8 5
```

South plays in five clubs and the defence begins with three rounds of spades. Clearly, the contract is defeated so long as East ruffs the third spade with the king of clubs. If West doubts his partner's willingness to ruff with an honour, he may lead the seven of spades on the third round—a loser instead of a winner.

Note that it would also be essential for East to ruff if he held Q x of trumps instead of K x. Similarly, a ruff with the queen from Q x x will promote a trick for partner's 10 x x, and a ruff with the ace from A x will gain when partner holds Q x over the declarer's king.

There are many occasions, too, when a ruff with a seemingly insignificant card will lead to a trump promotion. Suppose the trump suit is divided in this way:

Q 9 7

J 10 8   6 2

A K 5 4 3

West begins with three top winners in a side suit. Although he may know that South is going to overruff, East must not fail to insert the six of trumps. As the cards lie, this will create an extra trick for the defence.

Players are usually reluctant to ruff a winner with the ace of trumps, but this too may be very necessary:

K 8 7 4

J 9 3   A

Q 10 6 5 2

Assume, again, that West leads a winner to which neither East nor South can follow suit. So long as East is not too mean to part with his ace of trumps, the defenders will surely make two more trump tricks. If East discards, declarer may lead the first round of trumps from dummy and the singleton ace will beat the air.

Example 2

There are some engaging situations where the defenders can achieve a kind of long-distance promotion. Here West can see no other possibility for the defence:

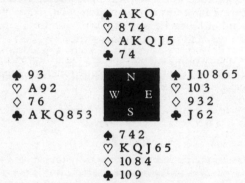

```
                    ♠ A K Q
                    ♡ 8 7 4
                    ◇ A K Q J 5
                    ♣ 7 4
    ♠ 9 3              N          ♠ J 10 8 6 5
    ♡ A 9 2                       ♡ 10 3
    ◇ 7 6          W       E      ◇ 9 3 2
    ♣ A K Q 8 5 3      S          ♣ J 6 2
                    ♠ 7 4 2
                    ♡ K Q J 6 5
                    ◇ 10 8 4
                    ♣ 10 9
```

North is the dealer and the bidding goes:

SOUTH	WEST	NORTH	EAST
—	—	1 ◇	pass
1 ♡	2 ♣	2 ♠	pass
3 ♡	pass	4 ♡	pass
pass	pass		

West begins with king and ace of clubs and can tell from the fall of the cards that his partner holds the missing club and that a third round will present the declarer with a ruff-and-discard. However, it is clear that this will not advance the declarer's cause and the only defence worth considering is to play a third round of clubs, preparing for a future trump promotion. When West wins the first round of hearts he plays a fourth club for his partner to ruff with the ten, and this establishes a trick for West's 9 x.

Sometimes the threat of a trump promotion will prevent the declarer from taking a normal combination finesse. Suppose that on the last hand the trump situation had been:

87

K 9 2   Q 3

A J 10 6 5 4

Left to himself, the declarer can keep the trump losers to one by the simple stratagem of taking two finesses. But if the defenders have established a position where East threatens to ruff a side suit, the declarer is in a dilemma. If he plays ace and another trump he will lose tricks to the queen and king, and if he finesses the ten he will be exposed to a trump promotion when East ruffs the side suit with the queen.

Example 3

Some remarkable effects can be achieved when the defenders are able to organize a double trump promotion. A declarer who has a strong trump holding such as K Q J 10 x x, with a singleton opposite, may easily lose two tricks if he has to overruff twice with the ten and jack. In this example a defender with just A 5 2 in the trump suit was able to promote a trick for the 5!

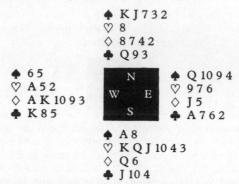

    ♠ K J 7 3 2
    ♡ 8
    ◇ 8 7 4 2
    ♣ Q 9 3

♠ 6 5   ♠ Q 10 9 4
♡ A 5 2   ♡ 9 7 6
◇ A K 10 9 3   ◇ J 5
♣ K 8 5   ♣ A 7 6 2

    ♠ A 8
    ♡ K Q J 10 4 3
    ◇ Q 6
    ♣ J 10 4

With both sides vulnerable, the bidding went:

SOUTH	WEST	NORTH	EAST
1 ♡	2 ◇	pass	pass
2 ♡	pass	pass	pass

West won the first two tricks with the king and ace of diamonds, then played a third diamond. As there could be no advantage in discarding a spade or a club, East ruffed with the seven of hearts. South had no loser that he could usefully discard, so he overruffed with the ten of hearts and led the jack. West went straight in with the ace and led a fourth diamond. East ruffed with the nine of hearts and after South had overruffed again the position in the trump suit was:

       —

 5 2   —

    K 4 3

West's five of hearts was now a winner, and South went one down, losing two hearts, two diamonds and two clubs.

Example 4

In the examples so far, the declarer has overruffed because he had no obvious loser to discard. It is normally good play for the declarer to dispose of a certain loser in preference to overruffing when this may cost a trick. The defenders, on the other hand, must aim to cash top winners before inviting the uppercut. This may call for accurate timing.

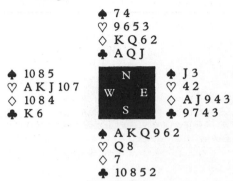

```
                  ♠ 7 4
                  ♡ 9 6 5 3
                  ◇ K Q 6 2
                  ♣ A Q J
  ♠ 10 8 5                      ♠ J 3
  ♡ A K J 10 7     N            ♡ 4 2
  ◇ 10 8 4       W   E          ◇ A J 9 4 3
  ♣ K 6            S            ♣ 9 7 4 3
                  ♠ A K Q 9 6 2
                  ♡ Q 8
                  ◇ 7
                  ♣ 10 8 5 2
```

South is in four spades and West leads the king of hearts. East begins an echo with the four, so that even if South drops the queen West will know, since the two is missing, that he can cash a second heart. (East would not have dropped the four from 8 4 2.) However, it would be a fatal error for West to continue with the ace of hearts. He sees the possibility of a trump promotion, should his partner hold the jack of spades or better, but two hearts and a trump will not beat the contract. Since there are no prospects of a trick in clubs, West must hope that his partner has the ace of diamonds.

It is essential to play a diamond at once, because otherwise South will discard a singleton diamond in preference to overruffing the third heart. So the play must go: king of hearts, diamond to the ace, heart return, and a third heart ruffed by the jack of spades. Against this sequence, there is nothing the declarer can do.

Before leaving this subject, it is worth noting a few combinations where the possibility of an uppercut may be overlooked.

```
                A 8 5 3
      K 10                     9
                Q J 7 6 4 2
```

If East has a chance to ruff with the nine, West's K 10 will be promoted.

                    A Q 5
        K 8 6   9
                    J 10 7 4 3 2

If this trump suit has been rebid by the declarer, West may think
that his king is dead; but there is a trick to be made if partner can
ruff with the nine, forcing declarer's ten.

Finally, there are some situations where an uppercut will at least
give the declarer a guess. This is the commonest:

                    K 8 5
        4 2   J 10 7
                    A Q 9 6 3

East is given the chance to ruff with the ten and South overruffs.
Evidently, as the cards lie, South can draw the remaining trumps
by playing off the king and ace, but from his point of view East
might have begun with 10 x and West with J x x. Thus he may
decide to play the ace and then finesse dummy's eight, losing to
the jack.

Example 5

An uppercut is not the only way of promoting trump tricks. Here the defenders may be able to take advantage of the positional factor:

K 8 6 4

A   Q 3

J 10 9 7 5 2

Assume that East, as a result of the early play, becomes void of a side suit. Then, when West wins with the ace of trumps, a further lead of the side suit will establish a trick for East's queen.

The same possibility arises when East holds J 10 x instead of Q x:

K 8 6 4

A   J 10 3

Q 9 7 5 2

Now East must be able to ruff a side suit early on. The ten forces declarer to overruff with the queen, and when West comes in with the ace of trumps he leads the same suit, establishing a trick for the jack.

The simplest form of trump promotion occurs when one of the defenders, being void of the suit led, has a chance to overruff the declarer. Sometimes a little foresight is necessary to bring about this situation. The following deal had quite an airing when the defensive play was first noted:

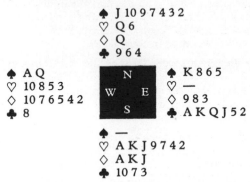

East opens one club and South overcalls with four hearts. This is passed out and West leads his singleton club. When East cashes a second club at trick two, West, looking ahead, must discard the queen of spades. On the third club he throws the ace of spades. East leads a spade at trick four and West is assured of a trump trick.

Imagination in Defence

In this final section we look at a number of defensive situations where it is necessary to place partner (or declarer) with specific cards. Once this effort of imagination has been achieved, the correct play is not too difficult.

Example 1

Here a well known position is presented in its simplest form:

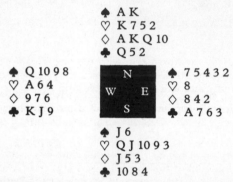

```
                    ♠ A K
                    ♡ K 7 5 2
                    ◇ A K Q 10
                    ♣ Q 5 2
  ♠ Q 10 9 8          N           ♠ 7 5 4 3 2
  ♡ A 6 4                          ♡ 8
  ◇ 9 7 6        W       E         ◇ 8 4 2
  ♣ K J 9              S           ♣ A 7 6 3
                    ♠ J 6
                    ♡ Q J 10 9 3
                    ◇ J 5 3
                    ♣ 10 8 4
```

North opens 2NT and South responds three hearts. (If transfer responses were being played, South would bid three diamonds, enabling the strong hand to be the declarer in hearts.) Over three hearts North bids three spades, indicating good support for hearts and a control in spades. South, obviously, declines the slam invitation and closes shop in four hearts.

West leads the ten of spades, won by dummy's king, and a heart is led to the queen and ace. Now it is very clear that West must look for the setting tricks in clubs, and the correct lead is the jack. Declarer may cover with the queen, but his ten is trapped on the next round.

There are many combinations where the correct card to lead when seeking for tricks is not so obvious. Sometimes it is necessary to prepare an unblock:

```
              10 6 5 2
     K 8 3                A J 7 4
              Q 9
```

Suppose that West deems it necessary to play for four tricks in this suit. He must lead the eight—no other card. East wins with the ace and returns the four, retaining the J 7 over dummy's 10 6. If West begins with the three, declarer can prevent the run of four tricks by declining later to cover the eight.

And suppose that East is the player who wants to attack this suit: then he must lead the ace and West must unblock the eight.

This is another common situation, again shown first in its simplest form:

A J 5

K 10 8 4   Q 7 6

9 3 2

If West is on lead he must begin with the ten. This holds the declarer to one trick. If West begins with the nine, South can play low from dummy and will have a double stop.

The same principle applies when the cards are like this:

A 9 5

K 8 3   Q 10 7 2

J 6 4

If East is attacking this suit he must lead the ten. Whether or not South covers, he makes only one trick.

Example 2

Just as there is usually a correct card to lead when a defender is looking for tricks in a suit, so there may be a correct card to lead when the object is not to give away tricks.

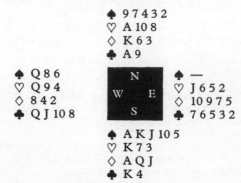

```
                    ♠ 9 7 4 3 2
                    ♡ A 10 8
                    ◊ K 6 3
                    ♣ A 9
  ♠ Q 8 6                           ♠ —
  ♡ Q 9 4          N                ♡ J 6 5 2
  ◊ 8 4 2        W   E              ◊ 10 9 7 5
  ♣ Q J 10 8       S                ♣ 7 6 5 3 2
                    ♠ A K J 10 5
                    ♡ K 7 3
                    ◊ A Q J
                    ♣ K 4
```

South plays in six spades and West leads the queen of clubs. When East shows out on the first round of trumps, South prepares for an elimination ending. He plays off two top spades, eliminates the diamonds and clubs, then throws West in with the queen of trumps.

Since a club would allow a ruff-and-discard, West must exit in hearts. The only good card is the queen.

If West had not held the nine in this example, the high card would still have been the best choice. Suppose the heart situation had been:

$$A 9 5$$

$$J 7 4 2 \qquad\qquad Q 6 3$$

$$K 10 8$$

If West (or East) has to lead this suit, the jack (or queen) at least gives the declarer a guess, because the lead might be from Q J x. If West leads the two, South will cap the queen with the king and will have no alternative but to finesse on the next round.

This position is less well known:

$$A J 6$$

$$K 10 4 3 \qquad\qquad Q 8 5$$

$$9 7 2$$

If West is obliged to lead this suit, and his life depends on not giving South two tricks, he must lead the king. Then South, even

if he is able to enter his hand on the second round and lead the
nine, must lose two tricks. If West begins with the ten, the jack will
be covered by the queen, and East's return of the suit (assuming
that he cannot safely exit in another suit) will give South a chance
to make two tricks by putting in the seven.

Example 3

There are numerous situations where the return of a particular
card provides the best chance to make the maximum number of
tricks later. Here East makes a pretty play:

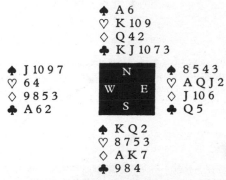

♠ A 6
♡ K 10 9
◇ Q 4 2
♣ K J 10 7 3

♠ J 10 9 7
♡ 6 4
◇ 9 8 5 3
♣ A 6 2

♠ 8 5 4 3
♡ A Q J 2
◇ J 10 6
♣ Q 5

♠ K Q 2
♡ 8 7 5 3
◇ A K 7
♣ 9 8 4

North opens one club and South, not belonging to the tribe that
considers it a capital offence to conceal a four-card major, responds
2NT. North raises to 3NT and West leads the jack of spades.
South wins in hand with the king and runs the nine of clubs to
East's queen.

Now, two fairly simple inferences are available to East: first, South
must hold the queen of spades (since partner led the jack); second,
that South does not hold the ace of clubs, for it would have been
normal to cash this card before taking the finesse.

It is true that South might hold K Q of spades alone, and in that
case a spade return would certainly ruin him. However, K Q x is
more likely, and in any case East has a better way to ensure the
declarer's defeat. If South held only three hearts, a lead of the
queen would be effective, but there is a stronger play—the two of
hearts. When West comes in with the ace of clubs he leads his
second heart and the defence makes two tricks in clubs and three
in hearts.

On other occasions the lead of an intermediate card is the best way to attack a suit. Here the best play is not obvious:

9 4

A J 8 7   10 6 3

K Q 5 2

Assume that West wishes to establish three tricks in this suit and that East has a side entry. To destroy the value of dummy's nine, West must lead the jack. Whether or not South takes the first trick, the defenders can establish three quick winners.

Example 4

The old advice to whist players, 'Second hand low, third hand high', is open to many exceptions. We have already seen some positions where second hand high is essential. On the following deal it would be foolish of East to part with his queen in third position:

♠ 10 8 3
♡ J 10 6
◇ Q 9 7 3
♣ A Q J

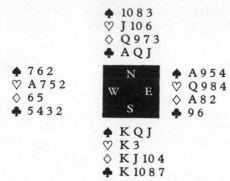

♠ 7 6 2   ♠ A 9 5 4
♡ A 7 5 2   ♡ Q 9 8 4
◇ 6 5   ◇ A 8 2
♣ 5 4 3 2   ♣ 9 6

♠ K Q J
♡ K 3
◇ K J 10 4
♣ K 10 8 7

South plays in 3NT and West stolidly leads fourth best from his longest and strongest suit—to wit, the two of hearts. (Most players would prefer a spade or a club, if no suit had been mentioned.) South plays the jack from dummy, and the fate of the hand depends on East's play at this point. If he puts on the queen he gives South a double stop. By playing the eight he establishes three heart tricks for the defence and beats the contract. To play the queen would be equally fatal if South held A K alone. If South has A x, then he has a double stop anyway.

It is often advisable to finesse against the dummy in preference to playing the highest card in third position.

10 6

A 9 5 4 2   Q 8 3

K J 7

West leads the four and dummy plays the six. East, defending against a no trump contract, should play the eight, not the queen. This holds the declarer to one trick, since after the eight has forced the jack the lead of the queen will pin dummy's ten. Of course, it *may* turn out that partner has led from A K x x x and declarer has only J x x. You have to consider, in the light of the bidding, whether this is a live possibility. The same kind of dilemma may arise when you hold K x x, in this type of situation:

J 4

A 8 6 2   K 9 3

Q 10 7 5

West leads the two and dummy plays low. More often than not, a finesse of the nine will save a trick, as it does here.

When partner has led from a short suit, it may be correct to retain a finesse position over the dummy.

Q 10 6 3

7 5 2   K J 8 4

A 9

West leads the seven against 3NT. The lead is obviously 'top of nothing' and when dummy plays low East must not put his jack under the hammer. By playing low he retains the chance of making two tricks later, with K J over dummy's Q 10.

Example 5

We conclude with three deals illustrating ways of attacking dummy's entries. Here the defenders use two well known stratagems:

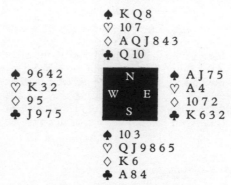

```
                    ♠ K Q 8
                    ♡ 10 7
                    ◇ A Q J 8 4 3
                    ♣ Q 10
   ♠ 9 6 4 2                         ♠ A J 7 5
   ♡ K 3 2            N              ♡ A 4
   ◇ 9 5          W       E          ◇ 10 7 2
   ♣ J 9 7 5          S              ♣ K 6 3 2
                    ♠ 10 3
                    ♡ Q J 9 8 6 5
                    ◇ K 6
                    ♣ A 8 4
```

North is the dealer and the bidding goes:

SOUTH	WEST	NORTH	EAST
—	—	1 ◇	pass
1 ♡	pass	2 ◇	pass
3 ♡	pass	4 ♡	pass
pass	pass		

West leads the nine of diamonds—not just as a 'safe' lead, but for a deliberate purpose. He knows that dummy has a long diamond suit and hopes, by playing this suit early on, to exhaust the declarer's holding and so spoil his communications.

South wins the first trick with the king of diamonds and leads a trump to the ten and ace. As there is a possibility that his partner has led a singleton, and in any case a diamond continuation must be the best line, East returns a diamond. When West wins the next trick in hearts he leads the two of spades, indicating a four-card suit. The queen is played from dummy and East wins with the ace.

East knows his partner can ruff the next diamond, but so can declarer. It is essential to return a spade, removing the entry from dummy. The jack of spades is safe, but a low spade is also good enough. Since there is still a trump out, South cannot make use of dummy's diamonds and eventually he must lose at least one trick in clubs.

Example 6

After a diamond lead, can the defenders beat four spades on the following deal? East can at least give the declarer a guess.

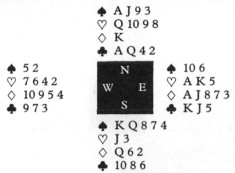

```
                    ♠ A J 9 3
                    ♡ Q 10 9 8
                    ◇ K
                    ♣ A Q 4 2
    ♠ 5 2              N            ♠ 10 6
    ♡ 7 6 4 2                       ♡ A K 5
    ◇ 10 9 5 4     W      E         ◇ A J 8 7 3
    ♣ 9 7 3            S            ♣ K J 5
                    ♠ K Q 8 7 4
                    ♡ J 3
                    ◇ Q 6 2
                    ♣ 10 8 6
```

At game all East deals and the bidding goes:

SOUTH	WEST	NORTH	EAST
—	—	—	1 ◇
pass	pass	dble	pass
1 ♠	pass	2 ♠	pass
3 ♠	pass	4 ♠	pass
pass	pass		

West should perhaps look for a trick in clubs, but instead he chooses the ten of diamonds. East wins the first trick and attempts to construct the declarer's hand. South is likely to hold five spades and at least three diamonds, since with five diamonds West would probably have raised the opening bid. If South has only five cards in hearts and clubs, East will have to hurry to establish a winner in clubs before the hearts have been developed.

Certainly a club is the right attack at trick two. East must still be careful in the choice of card. If partner has the ten it will make no difference which club East plays, but if declarer has the ten it may still be possible to cause him some anxiety. East may return a low club immediately, and South, holding 10 8 x, will have to decide whether to play the eight or the ten. If he puts in the eight, West's nine will force the queen and East will establish a trick in time. Alternatively, East may return the king of clubs at trick two and a low club later, giving declarer the same guess.

Note that it would be a mistake for East to lead the jack of clubs, either now or later. This is because the jack is one of the cards that the declarer will be worrying about. He will be inclined in any event to place East with the king, so if West leads the jack now and a low card later, South will make the right decision.

Example 7

The club attack on the last deal was necessary for reasons of timing rather than entry. The Merrimac coup, illustrated below, is more directly a communication play.

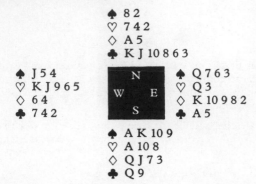

```
                ♠ 8 2
                ♡ 7 4 2
                ◇ A 5
                ♣ K J 10 8 6 3
♠ J 5 4                          ♠ Q 7 6 3
♡ K J 9 6 5         N             ♡ Q 3
◇ 6 4           W       E         ◇ K 10 9 8 2
♣ 7 4 2            S              ♣ A 5
                ♠ A K 10 9
                ♡ A 10 8
                ◇ Q J 7 3
                ♣ Q 9
```

South opens 1NT and North raises to 3NT. There is no point in mentioning the clubs, as North does not contemplate a final contract of five clubs.

West leads the six of hearts, East plays the queen and South must duck.

It may seem normal for East to return a heart, but against this defence South has no problem. He wins the second round (not minding if the suit should turn out to be 4—3) and knocks out the ace of clubs. So long as West does not hold five hearts and the club entry, the contract will be lay-down.

But East, confronted with the menace of the club suit in dummy, should not passively return a heart: he must lead a diamond to force out dummy's side entry. Moreover, he must lead the king of diamonds, not the ten. East will naturally hold up the ace of clubs for one round, and South will make at most eight tricks.

The sacrificial play of the king of diamonds is known as the Merrimac coup, following a historical parallel when a ship of that name was deliberately sunk in the bay of Santiago.

The play is often confused with the Deschapelles coup, named after a master of whist. The Deschapelles consists of the sacrifice of a high card to establish an entry for partner in this type of position:

A 4

Q 8 6   K 9 3 2

J 10 7 5

Imagine that East is on lead, that he has another entry card, and that it is vital to construct an entry for his partner. A low card will not achieve this, as South will put in the ten, but the King will assuredly force out the ace.

The term 'Deschapelles coup' is commonly used to describe both forms of play, but the distinction is surely worth preserving.